LIVING LIFE
TO THE FULL

AN INTRODUCTION TO
THE MORAL AND SOCIAL TEACHING
OF THE CATHOLIC CHURCH

David Albert Jones OP

© Fr David Albert Jones OP, 2001

ISBN 1-871217-35-0

Scripture quotations are taken
from the RSV Catholic edition

First published May 2001
Second edition July 2001

by the same author:
Christianity – An Introduction to the Catholic Faith

published by
Family Publications
77 Banbury Road, Oxford OX2 6LF
Tel: 01865 514408

CONTENTS

I What's the Point?

    Being happy   7
    Objective right and wrong   11
    Not just following rules   15
    Friendship with God   18

II How to Decide

    If it feels right, do it?   22
    Tough decisions   25
    Teaching with authority   28

III The Human Person

    Playing God?   33
    Innocent pleasures   37
    Loving the Truth   41

IV Society

    Honest relationships   45
    The power of the sword   49
    The cry of the poor   54
    The Kingdom of God   58

Suggested Further Reading   63

About this booklet

This booklet was produced in 2001 by the Oxford University Catholic Societies, in association with Family Publications. It has been distributed freely to the students of Oxford University thanks to the generosity of benefactors. It is intended to promote a wider understanding of the Catholic teaching on personal and social morality. Further copies are available from Oxford University Catholic Chaplaincy (for Oxford students) or direct from the publishers.

This is the second in a series of booklets explaining the Catholic faith. The first, ***Christianity: An Introduction to the Catholic Faith***, by the same author, was (in 1999) similarly given out to the students of Oxford University, and has also been distributed widely both nationally and internationally. It has been greatly acclaimed as an accurate yet concise and accessible summary of the Catholic Faith, and is already in its fourth edition.

The author has been a Dominican Friar since 1988. He is completing a doctorate in Moral Theology, and is currently working as the director of the Linacre Centre for Healthcare Ethics.

PREFACE

I have written this booklet as a brief introduction to the moral and social teaching of the Catholic Church, which shows us how to live the way of the Gospel. My writing has been strongly influenced by the wisdom of St Thomas Aquinas, one of the greatest Christian thinkers.

The booklet has four parts: the first two are about the Christian moral life *in general*, and introduce ideas such as 'natural law', 'virtue' and 'conscience'; parts three and four are about *particular issues*, such as 'medical ethics', 'the just war' and 'Catholic social teaching'.

This is not a book of answers to be memorised; rather, it hopes to introduce a fruitful *way of thinking*. It is not possible to deal with every topic explicitly and in detail in a small book such as this. The most important thing is to grasp the basic principles at work, and then think through particular questions for yourself.

David Albert Jones OP

Foreword

I am very glad to commend this booklet containing the moral and social teaching of the Catholic Church. Many people are sometimes confused concerning the moral teaching of the Church, and it is very good to have this simple booklet which sets out very clearly the manner in which we should live our lives and the norms which should guide our conduct.

I hope that *Living Life to the Full* will be read by very many people and help them to make sense of human life as they seek the happiness which is the true end of our life on earth.

+ Cormac Cardinal Murphy-O'Connor
Archbishop of Westminster

⁂ I ⁂
WHAT'S THE POINT?

BEING HAPPY

Blessed are the poor in spirit, for theirs is the kingdom of heaven. Blessed are those who mourn, for they shall be comforted. Blessed are the meek, for they shall inherit the earth. Blessed are those who hunger and thirst for justice, for they shall be satisfied. Matthew 5:3-6

We did not choose to exist; we find ourselves already existing amid a network of relationships and in the middle of a world we did not make. As we grow up, we 'come to ourselves' and find that we must live our own lives and make many decisions *for ourselves*. We have to decide what to *do*. Sometimes we just act out of habit, or do what everyone else is doing. At other times we are faced with choices: little choices, such as what to cook for supper, or what to buy for someone as a present; big choices, such as whether to abandon a job in the hope of something better, or whether a certain person is the right one to marry. The ability to decide things for ourselves is one of the things that mark human beings out from other animals. The Bible puts it in this way: 'It was the Lord who made human beings in the beginning, and he has left them in the hands of their own counsel' [*Sirach* 15:14].

But before we make a choice about something, we first have to be clear about *why* we are doing it: what is it that we are trying to achieve? What is the aim or purpose of our action? – I get the bus to go shopping. I go shopping to buy food. I buy food to eat. And why do I eat? I eat to stay alive; but eating is also a pleasure, a relaxation, and (normally) a social occasion. It is an important part of *human life*. But this brings us back further. What is it that makes sense of our *whole* life? What is it that we are seeking in and through all our various activities? What is it ultimately *all about*?

The answer to this question is **happiness** – or, perhaps better – *blessedness* or *human flourishing*. 'Happiness' in this sense means the *true end* of human life taken as a whole. Different people may organise their lives around different things. There are some people who organise their lives around food, those 'whose God is their belly' as Saint Paul puts it. Some people may not find any one thing that makes sense of their lives; but everyone realises that – wherever it is to be found – it is a good thing to find true happiness, and to find meaning in one's life.

The *ultimate* source of this meaning to human life is whatever principle or being it is that directs the whole universe, and gives life and shape to the natural world and to human history. If there *is* a meaning to life, then this meaning has to come from the Source of all life – and this is what Christians call the mystery of God. Those who believe in God can have confidence that human life *does* make sense, and that it *can* find fulfilment. The danger for those who do not explicitly believe in God is not so much that they will believe in *nothing* (for this requires a remarkable, if not perverse, kind of strength), but rather that they will believe in *anything*. A decline in traditional religion leads most people *not* into atheism, but into esoteric or 'alternative' cults and superstitions (which might give some degree of meaning to life). Otherwise they will be led into diversions, such as entertainment or recreational drugs (which might distract them from the lack of meaning in their lives).

The true happiness that we are all searching for will sometimes involve **suffering** or the willingness to suffer. The happiness we seek will not always be immediate, and it will not always be obvious. For instance, friendship, which is a part of happiness – and an image of our ultimate happiness in God – can sometimes be a cause of pain, even though of itself it gives pleasure. It is only through doing the right thing that we will become truly 'happy', in the sense of *being all that we can be*: flourishing and finding fulfilment as human beings: being *blessed*.

If, on the road to happiness, we sometimes have to

suffer something bad instead of *doing* something bad, this is never because we love suffering for its own sake. We may, for example, have to make an act of self-sacrifice; but this is always for our own good or the good of others. Suffering is sometimes a means, but it can never be an end, for our final hope is to find happiness, with others and for others, in God who is the source of all meaning and all life.

We are moved to happiness by a desiring-love, but we *find* happiness in a friendship-love, a love that comes from God. As a general principle, then, doing the right thing in our lives involves seeking happiness through *loving most strongly that which is most loveable*. It is because of this love that, despite their many sufferings, the saints are the happiest of people, for they live blessed, full and meaningful lives.

OBJECTIVE RIGHT AND WRONG

*And Jesus said to him, 'Why do you ask me about what is good? There is only One who is good. If you would enter life, keep the commandments.'
He said to him, 'Which?'
And Jesus said, 'You shall not kill, You shall not commit adultery, You shall not steal, You shall not bear false witness, Honour your father and mother, and, You shall love your neighbour as yourself'.*
Matthew 19:17–19

In matters of science, beliefs can be true or false, and theories can be more or less adequate. People may argue about matters of fact, but they are often able to find some way of testing who is right and who is wrong. Moral issues *seem* different. Arguments about abortion or animal experimentation, euthanasia or homosexuality, rarely convince anyone who was not previously convinced. As a result, many people think that value judgements are not about 'objective' reality – that is to say, they cannot be either 'true' or 'false'. Rather, they are thought of merely as expressions of emotion, or matters of taste (what someone happens to like or dislike). Furthermore, we know more nowadays about cultures that have very different customs from our own. Why should we be in a better position to judge than people in these cultures? How can we say that others are wrong?

Of course, it is easy to misunderstand another **culture**, and to assume that we have something to teach it but nothing to learn from it. It can be hard work to become familiar with the language, lifestyle and customs of others. Nevertheless, it can be done – and there are many books, articles and novels that give an accurate sense of other cultures. Indeed, we are able to come to understand other cultures *precisely* because of the many things that we all share as human beings – the importance of friendship and family, ideas of loyalty and betrayal, the experience of sickness and death, of joy and feasting. For example, although the *ways* people grieve are shaped by their cultures and their own personal histories, the *need* to grieve is universal. Once we recognise and are sensitive to such cultural differences, then we can become aware of the deeper universal similarities. Common moral judgements *are* thus possible, because we all share a common humanity.

When we learn to speak, it is in one particular **language**; but once we have learned it, we are able to understand truths that are common and universal. In a similar way, we learn what it is to be human by growing up within a specific human community with its own particular culture – but through this community we come to appreciate human values that are universal. This wider awareness enables us to identify and criticise practices within our own culture, or to compare our culture to other cultures. The abolition of slavery, for example, came about because people were not trapped within their own culture. Slavery's opponents were able to appeal to the transcendent value of human freedom, and so to criticise their own local prejudices and argue for a better way of doing things.

Some basic understanding of right and wrong is common to all mature human beings, and is what the Catholic tradition calls the **Natural Law**; it is in this sense that Catholics understand the following words of St Paul: 'When Pagans, who do not have the Law, do by nature what the Law requires, they show that what the Law requires is written on their hearts.' [*Romans* 2:14–15]

Of course, while almost everyone agrees about the basic principles of human action, the closer we get to particular actions, the more room there is for disagreement. Although moral judgements may be either true or false, they are not always *obvious* or self-evident. The arguments sometimes need to be very subtle, and the feelings they arouse can be powerful. People are often unwilling to change their own way of life, and can become attached to doing something that is wrong simply because it is pleasant or convenient. Hence moral debates are often over-emotional. All customs and actions need to be judged by the measure of the Natural Law, which can be discovered by reasoned reflection on the meaning of human life.

The Bible teaches us many new things about the moral

LIVING LIFE TO THE FULL

life, concerning forgiveness and the friendship of God (see page eighteen, below). However, at the same time it reminds us of those basic universal truths that, in principle, we could discover for ourselves, but for which we need a reliable guide. These truths are present in the Law that God gave to Moses, especially in the heart of that Law, the **Ten Commandments**:

1. Do not worship false gods.
2. Do not abuse the name of God.
3. Keep the Sabbath day as a holy day.
4. Honour your father and your mother.
5. Do not kill.
6. Do not commit adultery.
7. Do not steal.
8. Do not lie.
9. Do not desire to possess your neighbour's wife.
10. Do not desire to possess anything that belongs to your neighbour. [*Exodus* 20:2–17; *Deuteronomy* 5:6–21]

NOT JUST FOLLOWING RULES

And Jesus said to them, 'Have you never read what David did, when he was in need and was hungry, he and those who were with him: how he entered the house of God, when Abiathar was high priest, and ate the bread of the Presence, which it is not lawful for any but the priests to eat, and also gave it to those who were with him?' And he said to them, 'The Sabbath was made for man, not man for the Sabbath'.   Mark 2:25–27

There are some actions and customs that distort or destroy that which is good and valuable in human life. That is why we need **rules** like the Ten Commandments – to stop us from doing harm to ourselves and to others. However, rules on their own are not sufficient. – How do we know if the rule applies? Is there a rule that tells us when *every* rule applies? And how do we know when to apply *this* rule? Even with negative rules like 'Do not steal', it is not always obvious what *counts* as stealing. What happens when someone is in great need – for instance, in an emergency? What about borrowing and not returning? If a deal is unfair must it still be honoured? There are many fringe cases where it takes a wise and experienced person to judge whether a particular case is an example of stealing, and therefore forbidden by the commandment.

If this is true of the negative rules, then it is even more true of the positive commandments. 'Honour your father and your mother'. But how? When? To what extent? Does this rule mean that children must always obey their parents? If not, what are the exceptions? There cannot be a rule for every one of these questions. So rules are not enough on their own: they need a person who has an understanding of what the rules are for, what values they protect, and when they apply.

Furthermore, if we are to do the right thing, then we need more than simply an understanding of what is at stake. We must also be **good people**. An ungrateful son might refuse to go to a family event, in order to dishonour his mother and father, perhaps because he wants to make a show of his independence. Likewise, someone might steal while knowing full well that this action would cause great suffering; they might regret the fact, but be too greedy to return what was stolen. Another person might want very much to do the right thing, and see the attraction of doing it, but be too frightened of the consequences.

In order to do the right thing in a given situation, it is not enough to know the rules; we need good dispositions of character – what the Christian tradition (following the ancient Greek philosophers) calls the **virtues**. We need *practical wisdom*, so as to know what values are at stake, and what rules apply. We need to be *just* and fair-minded so that we are inclined to give people their due. Finally, we need to be *brave* in the face of danger, and *temperate* in the face of desire, so that fear or desire do not prevent us from doing the right thing. These four virtues – Practical Wisdom (known as 'Prudence'), Justice, Courage and Temperance – are called the **'cardinal' virtues** (from a Latin word, *cardo*, that means 'hinge'). They are the hinges on which good character hangs.

Rules and virtues work together: a virtuous person will understand the true meaning of the rules and be able to apply them. Virtues are like the skills of a musician or an athlete; they can be cultivated by practice and hard work, and become a sort of second nature, enabling the person who has them to perform well. On the other hand, virtues differ from skills in that skills make for a good *performance* whereas virtues make for a good *person* (it is possible to be a good performer without being a good person: a 'virtuoso' on the violin might be a person bereft of moral goodness). In the end, it is only the virtuous person who is good – the one who is wise, just, courageous and temperate.

Some people are not virtuous simply because they are immature, and have not yet developed their character. This is commonly true of young people, but it is also true of older people who have not taken sufficient responsibility for their own lives. At the other extreme, it is possible to have a stable and developed character, but one that is disposed towards a *distorted* or *corrupted* vision of the good life. This is much worse than simply being ignorant or immature. Bad dispositions of character, formed by deliberate acts, are called **vices**. The virtues act together in harmony, but the vices pull in different directions: you can be bad through being too assertive, or by not being assertive enough. A list can be made of the various vices that are opposed to the cardinal virtues – folly or cunning, injustice or self-destructiveness, cowardice or rashness, greediness or puritanism. However, the most famous list of vices in the Christian tradition is the **Seven Deadly Sins**: Pride, Envy, Anger, Apathy (Sloth), Avarice, Gluttony and Lust.

FRIENDSHIP WITH GOD

Greater love has no man than this: that he lay down his life for his friends. You are my friends if you do what I command you. No longer do I call you servants, for the servant does not know what his master is doing; but I have called you friends, for all that I have heard from my Father I have made known to you. [John 15:13–15]

What has been said so far – about happiness, natural law and the virtues – is only the beginning. We have not yet reached the heart of the Gospel message; for no purely *natural* account of human life will be sufficient to capture the true destiny of human beings. Even the deepest and most important elements of human life – married love, friendship, the search for wisdom – are not the end. For human beings have a capacity and a **destiny** which exceed any created source of fulfilment. We were made 'in the image of God', and our ultimate happiness lies in nothing less than finding peace in God. St Augustine once wrote: 'You made us for yourself, O Lord, and our hearts are restless until they rest in you'.

Furthermore, even natural justice is difficult for us to maintain on our own; even the best systems of justice are not free from corruption, and indeed in many countries corruption is not even disguised. Every nation has its underside, its forgotten past or hidden present: blood money, slave trading, questionable wars fought for dubious motives. Every nation knows its 'haves' and its 'have-nots', its selfishness, deception and political intrigue. However, one cannot trace this back to poor education and ignorance alone. There is something *disordered* within each one of us: a weakness and a flaw that we cannot fix on our own. This is due to an alienation from God – a state that we exist in from the moment we are conceived. This is what Christians call **original sin**.

So we have a double need: only God can give us a share in the Life that will bring us perfect happiness, and only God can bring order to the disorder within us. This double need was shown to us by the coming of Jesus, our

LIVING LIFE TO THE FULL

Saviour. Jesus preached mercy, healed people who were sick or troubled by evil spirits, and forgave sins. When he was executed, it was the clearest sign of how deeply sick the world is. The chief priests, the Roman governor, the people of the city, even one of his own disciples, all conspired to arrest, torture and murder him, though he was innocent of any crime. Jesus was 'dangerous' because he could not be tamed or manipulated. He showed the fierce mercy of God.

When Jesus rose from the dead, this showed that God the Father accepted the gift of his Son's life, as the basis for a **New Covenant** with mankind to answer this double need. Jesus in turn promised the Holy Spirit would come, to be the giver of new life for his disciples. The help we need from God is God himself – the Holy Spirit, given to inspire us and make us new. We call the presence of the Holy Spirit in us 'grace', a word that means 'free gift'.

The Christian life, then, is not just a life of law and virtue in pursuit of happiness; it is also a *friendship with God*. It may be objected that friendship is only truly possible between equals, and that no one can be equal with God. However, God *humbled himself* and became human, like us, so that we could have a share in his own life – and, therefore, a sort of equality, by being his 'adopted' sons and daughters. In this way we can now have a new dignity and freedom as God's own children.

The moral life of the Christian, then, is not only

about education in virtue. It is also a *drama* of sin and the grace of God. We have been rescued by God from the trouble we have brought upon ourselves by original sin and our own personal sins, and have been given a new way of life. That is why pride and an unforgiving attitude are so dangerous for the Christian: pride stops us from recognising our own need; a failure to forgive others cuts us off from the mercy that God wishes to show us also. Our help comes from God, not from ourselves. Mercy is shown to us; we must show mercy to others. Jesus himself taught us to pray, 'Forgive us our trespasses, as we forgive those who trespass against us' [*Matthew* 6:12]. If we act otherwise, then we resist or reject the friendship of God.

This new way of life, bestowed on us by God in the sacrament of baptism, brings with it those special virtues that give the Christian life its very shape. First comes *faith*, the gift that enables us to believe what God has revealed. Next comes *hope*, by which we entrust our lives to God. Finally, and most importantly, comes *love* – love for God and for others. These virtues, which make us not only good but *holy*, are called the **Theological Virtues** [see *1 Corinthians* 13]. Along with these inspired virtues, God also gives particular gifts to make us responsive to the promptings of the Holy Spirit within us. The Church lists seven such **Gifts of the Holy Spirit**: Wisdom, Understanding, Counsel, Courage, Knowledge, Piety and Fear of the Lord [*Isaiah* 11:2].

❖ II ❖

How to Decide

IF IT FEELS RIGHT, DO IT?

The eye is the lamp of the body. So, if your eye is sound, your whole body will be full of light; but if your eye is not sound, your whole body will be full of darkness. If then the light in you is darkness, how great is the darkness!   Matthew 6:22–23

It is part of the dignity of being human that we have the **freedom** to decide for ourselves how to act. Rather than limiting our freedom, the Gospel and the Holy Spirit actually *enable* it; they bring us a new and deeper freedom which allows us to liberate ourselves from the misery of sin. Natural law, the cardinal and theological virtues, and the gifts of the Holy Spirit provide a wide scope of action for us. There are many things we *might* do, countless ways to live out the Christian life. Not every way of life will be open to us; but the options are nearly always wider than we think, and it remains for us to take one particular path.

The dignity of human and Christian freedom is something that must always be respected. A person can help someone make a decision through support, advice or example, but that person cannot make up their mind for them. All of us must learn to take responsibility for our own decisions and make them as best we can.

Conscience is our considered *judgement* about whether a particular action, committed or merely contemplated, is good or bad. It is never right to act against our conscience for reasons of weakness or cowardice; nor is it proper to encourage others to act against theirs – 'It is right not to do anything that makes your brother stumble' [*Romans* 14:21]. In this sense the judgement of conscience must always be respected.

But our conscience can also get things wrong. Just because I myself judge that this particular action ought to be done (or avoided) here and now, it does not follow that I have necessarily made the right decision. Our judgements about what to do must be informed by the virtue of prudence (practical wisdom), by self-knowledge and knowledge of the circumstances, by seeking advice and by being open to correction. If someone tries hard to make the right decision, but gets it wrong, then the mistake might well be innocent; a good person will sometimes do bad things out of ignorance. But *some* ignorance results from our own ill will. People who make a habit of taking advantage of others, for example, will soon stop feeling pangs of conscience for doing so. Their view of right and wrong will become darkened, and it will become more difficult for them to see things clearly. When this happens, ignorance is no longer a legitimate excuse.

On the other hand, although merely doing what feels right *may* be the right thing to do, we should always think through the implications and the consequences of our actions. Sometimes it will be important to overcome our initial feelings. Acting without thought and without shame is not a sign of strength, but a sign of weakness, laziness or cowardice.

Furthermore, if we are given responsibility over others, we must sometimes *discipline* them regardless of their willingness to accept this. For instance, a worker who causes offence by racist jokes should be reprimanded, not just for his own sake, but also for the sake of his colleagues, and for the common good. The Gospel tells us that correction among equals – colleagues, co-workers, classmates – is also a responsibility; but such fraternal correction will be effective only if the person corrected is willing to *accept* criticism – so we ought to think carefully about when and how to approach that person. If it seems unlikely that a person will change, then we should weigh the value of trying to correct them against the trouble it might cause. However, if someone comes to us looking for approval which we cannot give, then we must overcome our cowardice or embarrassment and say what needs to be said. Fraternal correction, when it is done well, is an act of love.

TOUGH DECISIONS

Then Jesus said to them, 'My soul is very sorrowful, even to death; remain here, and watch with me'. And going a little farther he fell on his face and prayed, 'My Father, if it be possible, let this cup pass from me; nevertheless, not as I will, but as thou wilt'. Matthew 26:38–39

The Christian life, inspired by the Holy Spirit, is not just about *occasional* difficult choices. It is about the attitude or spirit behind *all* our acts, great and small. However, in this life we walk by faith rather than by sight, and there are many things we do not understand. We are sometimes faced with difficult decisions and find ourselves at a loss as to what we should do.

Decisions may be difficult for different reasons. First there are decisions that are *intellectually* difficult. We must have the courage to act on our limited knowledge, for inactivity is also a decision in itself. We must act as best we can and leave it to God to bring good from our mistakes. We cannot be expected to see things as God sees them.

Other decisions are *emotionally* difficult: we have to face the prospect of suffering, or resist the attraction of immediate pleasures. These difficulties are just as real as those of moral quandaries.

Finally, there are many decisions that are difficult in *both* ways: they are perplexing *and* emotionally difficult. The difficulty of telling someone that their loved one has died is, in part, a matter of knowing what to say; but it is mainly the difficulty of sharing emotional distress.

We can grapple with these difficulties, but they do not always have a 'perfect' solution that will make everyone happy. Thus they give rise to the temptation to accept a false solution that *appears* to make everything 'all right', if only we are willing to do some little act of wickedness. This false promise has even been codified into a system called **proportionalism**, by which *any* act can be allowed if there is a 'proportionate reason' for doing it; that is, a strong enough motive. 'Proportionalism' is a system that is incompatible with the Church's tradition. It was condemned by Pope John Paul II in 1993, in an 'encyclical' – a letter to the whole Church – called *Veritatis Splendor* ['The Splendour of Truth']. There are certain actions we must exclude *altogether* because they are things that a virtuous person would never do: betray the faith; lie; murder; steal; commit adultery. The Catholic Church calls such actions *intrinsically bad*, and says that it is always wrong to do evil in order that good may come of it [*Romans* 3:8].

Sometimes we are faced with a dilemma in which, whatever we do, someone will be harmed. In such situations we should be guided by the **principle of double**

effect: side effects should be assessed differently from the effect that we are aiming to bring about. Adopting the lesser of two evils is a principle which applies *only* to weighing side effects, given that an action is acceptable in itself.

For example, in the case of an 'ectopic pregnancy' – when the embryo has implanted in the wrong place and the pregnancy threatens the life of the mother – the doctor may not respond with a deliberate attack on the child. However, he may remove the damaged organ from the woman, even if he knows that, as a side-effect, the child will die. Causing death *unintentionally* is very serious, but may be permitted in certain extreme circumstances. Murder, that is, the deliberate and *intended* killing of the innocent, is never justified, no matter how extreme the situation. It matters crucially whether the effect is 'direct' or 'indirect', that is, intended or unintended.

Many moral dilemmas involve **co-operation** with evil. Co-operation in common projects is an important social virtue, but it poses a problem when we find ourselves involved in someone else's wrongdoing. Should a doctor 'clerk in' women who are going to have abortions? Should a company trade with oppressive and unjust governments? Should a newspaper print letters expressing intolerant or inflammatory views? Acting in such a way that you share another person's wrongful aims is called *direct* or *formal co-operation*, and is always wrong. Doing what helps the person, but without sharing the wrongful aims, is called *indirect* or *material co-operation*, and this need not be immoral; however, material co-operation may be a cause of scandal, and non-co-operation can be an important 'prophetic' witness to call attention to an ongoing injustice.

Morality is not, however, only about *excluding* certain actions; we must above all try to do something *positive*. Following rules is not enough on its own to tell us what particular positive thing we should do: for this we need virtue, experience and imagination. The experience of trying to respect many different human values, together with a strong commitment never to betray any of these by doing wrong, makes us the sort of people who can face difficult situations well. It is the *virtuous* person who knows what to do in a difficult situation.

TEACHING WITH AUTHORITY

> *And when Jesus finished these sayings, the crowds were astonished at his teaching, for he taught them as one who had authority, and not as their scribes.* Matthew 7:28–29

What is the proper role for *authority* in morals? Authority does not mean the power to force someone to obey (as though the person obeying were just a well-trained animal). Authority, properly speaking, means that someone's word is itself a good reason for doing or believing something.

To give an example: Margaret is an authority on birds. Since she is very knowledgeable, it is reasonable to accept what she says on this subject. Occasionally she might make a mistake, and I might catch her out, but her word remains credible nonetheless. Some **expert authority** is like this, such as is the case with a wise counsellor. But there is another reason for having authorities on practical matters: if a group of people is going to do something together, it is very useful to put someone in charge. Some things can only get done if someone has overall responsibility for doing them. This kind of **political authority**, which belongs to whoever is in charge, also gives us a good reason to act – for the sake of respecting the common order of society. However, this is not always an over-riding reason; we should never do things that we ourselves *know* to be wrong.

The authority of Jesus was not a political authority in this sense, nor was it the authority of an expert who knows his subject. Jesus had authority from God. The authority of God is not like human authority, for God *cannot* make mistakes. God is all goodness and all truth, so if God tells us to do something, then we know that it must be the right thing to do. We should obey God, *not* because God is greater and stronger than we are, but because God is the best guide to what will truly fulfil us.

The authority which the **Catholic Church** has to teach on moral matters is not just a human authority (based on knowledge from experience) or a political authority (because the Church is a society) – though she has these authorities as well. The authority of the Church to teach on moral matters comes directly from God, because the Church is founded on Jesus, who is God become man; and because the Holy Spirit, who is God present within us, continues to guide and guard the Church. When the Church teaches with her full authority, she teaches the word of God, which is, of its nature, true.

At the same time it is also important to stress that *not everything* that has been taught in the Catholic tradition has the same degree of authority. What has been taught solemnly by a pope or an ecumenical council representing the whole Catholic Church, or what has been taught always and everywhere by all the bishops, is certain, true and infallible. However, many of the Church's teachings do not fall into this category. Furthermore, the Church's understanding of the Gospel message has developed over time, under the guidance of the Holy Spirit. For instance, while slavery was never encouraged, the Church did at first tolerate it (the New Testament does not condemn the practice). Only later, in response to the appalling slave trade that developed in relatively modern times (from the sixteenth century), did the Church start to work actively for its complete abolition.

How then can we find out what is essential teaching and what is changeable? The **Creeds of the Church** concentrate on matters of faith, not on moral matters – because in the past the Church's moral teachings were not greatly disputed. Perhaps, in the future, creeds will be drawn up that explicitly involve moral truths. For now, there already exist some important Church documents on moral and social teaching; and, of course, we must also consider the moral and social teaching present in the Bible, as it is understood by the Catholic tradition. There are certain points that are so central to the Catholic moral tradition that they must be considered *essential* and *unchangeable*, such as the Christian virtues of faith, hope and love, and the absolute prohibition on adultery, killing the innocent, and worshipping false gods. In doubtful matters the first question to ask is not 'Do I agree with this teaching?' but rather 'Is this teaching from God?', and then 'How can I understand this teaching in the light of the whole tradition?'

If some proposition is only part of the changeable *expression* of the Gospel, then it *may* need to be re-expressed in some other way. However, even here, we must still give weight to the authority of the Church and support those who have the difficult job of leading. The Pope or bishop has a duty to make particular decisions for the sake of the common good – such as appointing pastors, disciplining erring theologians, or settling disputes concerning faith or morals. Although such actions may be changeable – unlike the Church's most solemn moral teaching – they must still be respected for their public, legal and positive force, and should always be obeyed as far as we are able.

III

THE HUMAN PERSON

PLAYING GOD?

And Jesus said to them, 'Whose likeness and inscription is this?' They said, 'Caesar's'.
Then he said to them, 'Render therefore to Caesar the things that are Caesar's, and to God the things that are God's'. Matthew 22:20–21

Every individual human being is a new creation, the result of a special intimate act of God. We each have a mother and a father, from whom we inherit our physical features – but our deepest nature, as free and spiritual beings, was created directly and immediately by God. God sustains and provides for us throughout our lives; however, we *think* of our status as creatures particularly when we think of our creation by, and our return to, God. For, as the Bible says, 'there is for all mankind one entrance into life, and a common departure' [*Wisdom* 7:6]. So it is particularly the events of procreation and of bodily death that raise the deepest questions about our nature as human beings.

Ancient medicine was very hit-and-miss. Even when effective it was still very much the assistant to the body's own restorative powers. **Modern medicine** can do much more, but it has also extended its power over us. It is now possible to manipulate egg and sperm in a glass dish and bring about a conception in the laboratory. It is possible to test for defective genes, even in the womb, and it may soon be possible to change genetic characteristics at this stage. At the end of life, it is possible to sustain someone who has lost the ability to breathe, or to transplant organs so as to give patients a new lease of life. It is also possible to use technology to kill someone, if that is what we choose to permit. These possibilities lead to special questions in the area known as medical ethics or **bioethics**.

The Catholic tradition is strongly committed to the progress of medicine. In fact, the Catholic Church is the largest provider of healthcare in the world. Medicine promotes the good of bodily health. This is not only a means to enable us to do things: good health is actually an *intrinsic* part of a flourishing human life.

However, this good must be pursued in a way that also respects the other goods of the human person. For example, healthcare must be *just*, which means that it should be distributed fairly, and medical knowledge should never be used to injure or to kill. **Abortion** kills an unborn child and is always an act of injustice. It is also damaging to the mother physically, psychologically and morally. **Suicide** is wrong because it is a failure properly to value one's life and live it to the full, even when things are difficult; it is a failure to accept death only from God's hand, such that the end, like the beginning, is a divine gift. **Euthanasia** – deliberate killing by act or omission – is worse than suicide. It involves the decision that killing a particular (old, ill or disabled) person would count as 'helping', because *we* decide that he or she would be 'better off dead'. If this becomes accepted by society, it will also threaten vulnerable people, by making them believe they are a burden to others.

Infertility is a great affliction, and it is right that medicine should seek to cure it, so couples can have children of their own. However, many new reproductive technologies do not *cure* infertility or *assist* the act of procreation, but instead *replace* it. A 'test-tube baby' is not conceived as a result of lovemaking. Worse still, the child who is born will be only one among a large number of embryos conceived – many of whom are thrown away or used in experimentation. This is killing on a huge scale. Proper treatment of infertility includes fertility drugs, tubal surgery and other forms of treatment that retain the link between the couple's lovemaking and the child's conception, and do not destroy embryonic human lives.

In the future, human embryos may also come into existence by **cloning**: by transplanting the nucleus of an adult's cell into a human egg. Cloning sheep and other mammals has a high failure rate, and a human being could only be cloned at the cost of hundreds of lives. Even if it became safe, it would still be unfair deliberately to bring a child into the world without a natural mother and father. Much worse than 'reproductive' cloning is the so-called 'therapeutic' cloning of embryos, so as to harvest their valuable stem cells. This is, in effect, breeding human beings for slaughter.

The attempt to alter someone's genetic make-up is legitimate in principle, when it corrects some defect, just as a disability may be corrected by surgery. However, while it is a good thing to seek to improve the health of future generations (for instance, by protecting the quality of the environment), our scientific understanding is not mature enough to risk 'germ-line' **gene therapy**: altering genes that will be passed on from generation to generation. **Eugenics** – seeking to enforce 'genetic health' – threatens people's freedom to marry whom they wish, and have children of their own. It promotes *prejudice* against anyone who suffers from genetic defects, especially unborn children. **Prenatal screening**, when performed in order to selectively kill the unborn, along with policies which prevent the 'genetically defective' from having children, are great evils. Policies based on the strong's fear of the weak are destructive of a just society.

INNOCENT PLEASURES

The father said, 'Bring the fatted calf and kill it, and let us eat and make merry; for this my son was dead, and is alive again; he was lost, and is found'. And they began to make merry. Now his elder son was in the field; and as he came and drew near to the house, he heard music and dancing. Luke 15:23–25

In general, what is pleasant is good for us, and what is painful is bad (though pain does serve the good purpose of alerting us to harm). However, balancing our instinctive desire for pleasure and our fear of pain is not enough to guide a mature human being. To reach true happiness we must sometimes endure pain or sacrifice pleasure. This takes courage, which is not the absence of fear, but rather the ability to do the right thing without letting fear paralyse us. Everyone needs courage to live well and to endure or to overcome hardships.

Modern society, through advertising and peer pressure, is constantly pushing us to seek unlimited pleasure in music and entertainment, food and drink, sex and drugs. In order to keep our balance we must cultivate the sort of desires that will actually help us to find happiness. It is good to take pleasure in **food and drink**, and to enjoy feasting on special occasions; but we should moderate our diet for the sake of our health. Furthermore, life is more important than food and drink, and we should sometimes eat less in order to become more aware of the needs of others, and more aware of our own dependence upon God. This is called 'fasting'.

Emotional over-dependence on eating sweets, drinking alcohol or smoking cigarettes is a kind of *enslavement* and, as such, it is something from which we should wish to be free. Occasional **smoking** is an innocent pleasure, but most people are unable to smoke only occasionally. Taking recreational **drugs** has two serious risks: the danger of becoming addicted, and the possibility of damaging our physical or mental health. These risks vary tremendously depending on the drug. Moreover, the rule of law is essential to the good of any society, and laws should not be broken without good reason. Getting a quick 'high' is not a good reason, and even buying soft drugs lends support to a criminal economy.

Sexual desire involves our personality more strongly than the other forms of desire. Both married and single people need the virtue of **chastity** to integrate it into their lives. The origin and purpose of sexual desire is to create a bond between a man and a woman, so that they can bear and raise their children together. Yet, because of the widespread use of contraceptives, and a culture dominated by pleasure seeking, many people have no sense that there is anything seriously wrong with a casual sexual liaison, so long as it is consensual and does not betray an existing relationship. But such actions *are* harmful, because they endanger the future welfare of a child who might be conceived, because they pose a risk to health and emotional stability, and because they corrupt the essential and intrinsic meaning of sexual intimacy.

Sexual love has its own distinctive character. It finds fulfilment not just in *any* kind of friendship, but only through a *particular* kind of relationship. Its meaning is found within the sort of relationship that could produce and welcome children, i.e. **marriage** that is free, mature, committed, heterosexual and open to new life. However, if a couple does happen to be infertile, this does not in itself undermine the meaning of marriage. The Catholic tradition strongly defends marriage, and the good of sexual desire and sexual pleasure within marriage, but also affirms that it *is* possible, with the help of God, to live a happy life without being married. The Church has always especially honoured those people who sacrifice married life in order to dedicate themselves to prayer or preaching. This is called **celibacy**. In our society, those who are not free or inclined to marriage are given very little support in living a happy life without sexual companionship. The Church must offer that support to **single people**; but it must also be faithful to the truth that marriage is the only fitting context for sexual expression, because sexual desire is internally and naturally ordered towards a full marital relationship. The natural and symbolic link between lovemaking and procreation is the reason why the Catholic Church has consistently opposed sodomy and masturbation.

It is good for couples to be responsible and plan their families in accordance with their circumstances; and this can be done very effectively by *abstaining* from making love during the period in a woman's menstrual cycle when she is fertile (this is called **'Natural Family Planning'**, or NFP). Contraceptive drugs or condoms, however, are barriers that prevent perfect union, and impose a symbolic as well as a physical sterility. Sadly, many Catholics practise contraception, often wrongly believing that this is the only way they can be responsible parents. Despite this, the Church has continually taught that contraception is contrary to the true meaning of sexual love.

'Living the good life' means *acting* well, and enjoying good things; pleasure, though, is merely about *feeling* good – it can mislead us, and an excessive desire for it can be destructive. On the other hand, despising the good things that God has created, or being cold towards them, is also disordered. Puritanism and over-indulgence are two opposite extremes, but both are equally incompatible with the Gospel message. Virtue consists in taking pleasure in the right things *to the right extent*. In order to achieve personal integration, social justice and care for our environment, we must be able to find joy and pleasure in a *simple* way of life.

LOVING THE TRUTH

> *Jesus answered, 'You say that I am a king. For this I was born, and for this I have come into the world, to bear witness to the truth. Everyone who is of the truth hears my voice.'*
> *Pilate said to him, 'What is truth?'* John 18:37–38

A human being is not just a mind *using* a body. Our understanding is not separate from our bodily life, but infuses it completely. Even simple physical pleasures, such as eating, are mingled with the pleasures of companionship or conversation, and also with how we think about the food. Food is not only sweet or salty, but is also characteristic of a particular place or culture. It can be interesting or dull, comforting or adventurous. No human desire is *purely* animal; equally, no human desire is *purely* intellectual. A chess player will sweat if the game becomes tense; a great discovery will set the scientist's heart pounding. As *social* animals, much of our communicating is not, in fact, about passing on information, so much as enjoying someone else's company, or establishing a relationship. Yet, as *thinking* animals, the *truth* itself is valuable to us.

All truth comes from God. Like an artist or a designer, God has always had a vision of his intended creation. For this reason the universe is intelligible, because it was created in accordance with God's plan. Human beings were created in God's image, with the ability to know and to learn. Thus, when our minds grasp a truth about the universe, we are, in some small way, coming to know the mind of God. In this sense, God *is* Truth.

The search for truth, and the delight in thinking about and sharing the truth, is a basic part of human happiness. However, since learning is hard work and takes time, every society allows some of its members to devote themselves especially to learning, both for their own sake and for the common good. **Science** can be useful for making things, for example; but it is first of all a good thing *in itself*: it makes us a people with understanding. Science, research and education are important aspects of life; but like all good things they must be pursued in the right way. Scientists and scholars are sometimes tempted to 'cheat' and invent evidence for something that they want to believe is true, but which is not yet proven. It is never right to lie in the pursuit of truth, for this undermines our capacity to seek and value that truth. It is worse still to lie, or steal other people's ideas, for the sake of status, fame or wealth. If we are concerned about 'copyright', our first question should not be 'Is this legal?' but rather 'Is this just and honest?'

In **education**, especially that of children, it is often necessary to simplify a complicated idea, and only add qualifications at a later stage, so that the student can then see the whole picture. However, it is wrong to present pictures, models and half-truths as though they were the whole truth, and it is worse still to persuade someone to believe something false. There is nothing wrong with telling stories; but when a child is old enough, he or she should be taught how to make distinctions between the different sorts of story – fable, epic and history. Simplifying without falsifying is very difficult; but falsification defeats the true purpose of education and fails to respect the mind of the learner.

If sharing the truth is sometimes a problem for scientists and teachers, it can be far worse in the worlds of **journalism**, **politics** and **advertising**. Though there are responsible editors and journalists, politicians of personal integrity, and advertising agents with moral sensitivity, it is particularly difficult to maintain and protect certain moral principles in these environments. Indeed, if the first aim in these fields is to entertain, rule or persuade, rather than to share the truth and serve society, then it takes a strong personal commitment for an individual to keep hold of the value of truth in itself. If we fail to value truth, then we begin to turn away from God.

In our personal lives we tell jokes and tall stories and family myths without taking these too seriously. However, we also keep secrets: sometimes for very good reasons, sometimes to cover up something we should not be doing. It is difficult to keep a secret without lying. If we are to avoid lying, then we need the virtues of **discretion** and **tact**, so that we can remain silent about what we should not say, and say well those things that are difficult to express. Conventional phrases, used as excuses or in casual speech, are sometimes not meant to be taken literally, but even here we should be careful not to cultivate bad habits and slip into dishonesty. 'White lies' are always failures to respect the truth, whatever our good intentions, and they can easily lead to messy complications –

> 'Oh, what a tangled web we weave
> When first we practise to deceive'.

❈ IV ❈
SOCIETY

HONEST RELATIONSHIPS

But from the beginning of creation, 'God made them male and female'. For this reason 'a man shall leave his father and mother and be joined to his wife, and the two shall become one flesh'. So they are no longer two but one flesh. What therefore God has joined together, let not man put asunder.

Mark 10:6–9

We come into the world through the union of our mother and father. Even if we do not know either of our parents, they are still part of our story and identity. We learn from our immediate family how to speak and relate to others – from our parents or guardians, brothers and sisters.

Family ties, especially those between parents and children, and brothers and sisters, are very strong by nature. This does not mean that we always get on easily with our families. The more we share ourselves with others, the more easily we can hurt one another. With friends we can put on a good show, but our family sees us as we are – at our worst, as well as at our best. Family ties are not freely chosen by us, but they are *part* of us, whether we like it or not; and the first task of a human being is to learn to live in and with his or her family. It is in this environment that we learn to relate to others and come to mature self-knowledge.

Becoming a parent gives both the mother and the father a new responsibility. Even if the child was unforeseen, he or she is still the child of these two people. **Parenthood** is a natural role, which – like being human itself – shapes our interests and duties. It is not only a matter of supplying a child's material needs, but also of accepting them as a person and trying to develop a good relationship through which both parent and child can develop. It is wrong to set out to conceive a child if both the mother and the father are genuinely unable to cope with the responsibilities of parenthood; but, once conceived, every child must be cherished.

Others can help us in the job of **rearing and educating** – relatives, childminders, teachers – but it is the duty, and therefore the *right*, of parents first and foremost to bring up their child according to their own understanding. Children also have a duty to obey and learn from their parents. The city, tribe or state has no right to come between parent and child unless the child is in serious danger. Sometimes a parent who cannot cope will give up a child for **adoption**; and accepting a child for adoption is a great act of love. While being brought up by another family makes for difficulties, especially during adolescence when the child is trying to establish his or her own identity, it is certainly better than being brought up in an institution without any sense of belonging to a family.

We all grow up in a family, and may eventually find someone we wish to live with as husband or wife, in order to start a family of our own. The Catholic Church recognises marriage as a human good common to all peoples, but sees **Christian marriage** as having an extra dimension – a lifelong sacramental bond. Jesus said that anyone who divorces and marries again is being unfaithful to the first and true marriage [*Mark* 10:11–12]. Separation may be necessary in extreme situations, but the Church does not recognise divorce as an option for baptised Christian spouses, if their marriage was fully consummated and valid. However, if there was something deficient from the beginning, then it might not have been a *valid* marriage; and, after investigation, the Church might give the couple a declaration of nullity, or 'annulment'. Then both partners would be free to marry others.

There is something noble in companionship between people of the same sex, and this is a blessing from God, but advocating the legal recognition of 'same-sex unions' seriously threatens the public understanding of marriage, the family and children, and further undermines the sanity of the common culture in the area of human sexuality. As argued earlier, sexual expression finds its proper human context *only* within the bond of marriage, and when sexual communion is open to the blessing of children; an infertile married couple may still be *open to* children, but the sterility of homosexual intercourse is an *essential aspect* of the kind of activity it is.

Extended family ties – with cousins, aunts and uncles – are less significant these days in modern Western societies like Britain. The state has taken over the provision of healthcare, education and public order, and has a much greater influence on our lives than it once did. Most people do not now work in family businesses. The idea of **loyalty** to an extended family has also been undermined by changes in the way we live. However, loyalty is still an important human virtue, and people do also get a sense of belonging from their profession, town, region, or particular 'sub-culture' (defined by religion, common interest or ethnic background). Loyalty can easily degenerate into unfairness or prejudice towards 'outsiders'. In order to be healthy, loyalty must always be combined with **openness** and generosity, so that the knowledge that we belong gives us the confidence to accept others.

It is important to be able to get on well with others in the workplace, because difficult personal relationships can make it very hard to work well together. Nonetheless, good business relations – *friendships of mutual usefulness* – are not true friendships. More important are the relationships we have with people whom we spontaneously like and whose company we enjoy. However, these *friendships of pleasant company*, important as they are for us, still do not answer our basic need for serious friendship. **True friendship**, something that we cannot have with more than a few people, involves a shared life of common commitment to the true good of one another. Aristotle called this the 'friendship of virtue'; St Aelred of Rievaulx called it 'spiritual friendship'. True friendship is a very great human good.

THE POWER OF THE SWORD

Pilate said to him, 'You will not speak to me? Do you not know that I have power to release you, and power to crucify you?' Jesus answered him, 'You would have no power over me if it had not been given you from above'. John 19:10–11

Humans are **social beings**; not only at the level of family or close friends, but also at the higher level of tribe, city or nation. This is not an unfortunate necessity, but is good, proper and natural to us. It allows some people to specialise in a trade or skill. It allows schools, sport and drama. The word civilisation comes from the Latin *civitas* – city or commonwealth. Many ancient and recent civilisations have been built on pride, ambition and injustice – but cities, as such, offer great opportunities for their inhabitants. The Bible talks of the corrupt city of Babylon, but it also talks of the holy city of Jerusalem.

Cities and nations need to give authority to particular people so they can make decisions and act effectively. The existence of **rulers** and **governments** is not itself an effect of our fall from innocence, but is a natural part of being human. There is, however, an aspect of political power that *is* a result of the Fall. Cities and governments now have the task of protecting people against the *violence of wrongdoers*. Without the threat of force a government would be powerless to act against murderers, robbers, bandits, terrorists or revolutionaries; stable society simply could not exist. A country also needs to be policed against violence and crime committed by its own citizens, and defended from enslavement or oppression by other nations. This power to protect the common good – by the use of force when necessary – is described by St Paul in these words: 'He who resists the authorities resists what God has appointed. For he [the one in authority] does not bear the sword in vain; he is the servant of God, to execute his wrath on the wrongdoer' [*Romans* 13:2–4].

The Christian tradition, then, has always upheld the **right of civil society to defend itself**. Although Christians initially refused to serve in pagan armies, the Church from the fourth century onwards encouraged its members to take responsible posts in society, and therefore to serve as magistrates and soldiers. Yet there have always been those, such as priests and monks, who saw any form of violence as incompatible with their personal calling – who spoke with a prophetic voice from outside society, like St John the Baptist. This is the legitimate place of **Christian pacifism**.

The mainstream Christian tradition certainly does not allow everything that goes on in the name of war. The bombing of innocent civilians, the torture of prisoners to obtain information, the use of indiscriminate weapons (such as landmines, poison gas, napalm, and biological or nuclear weapons), or the funding of anti-government terrorists, are not justifiable acts of war but are themselves acts of injustice. They reduce us to the level of those we fight against. The only sort of war that a person of integrity should support (the **just war**) is one that:

- is the last resort to oppose a great evil
- is not an excessive reaction out of all proportion to the evil it opposes
- is likely to be fought in a limited way, against soldiers rather than against the innocent
- has a clear aim and a reasonable chance of success
- is pursued by a legitimate political authority.

Christians should be cautious about going to war, because of our natural tendency to deceive ourselves about our 'pure' motives for doing things (for we also are sinners), and because we should treat all enemies as merely wayward friends. We should only fight when it is for the general good, for the sake of the people of the enemy state as well as for our own.

The use of force is also legitimate in **policing** and in the **punishment of criminals**, where it is used to protect people against harm or injustice. This does not mean that every injustice should be made illegal – for some laws are unworkable in practice, and some evils should be tolerated for the sake of relative freedom. For instance, adultery is always a bad thing, but it would hardly help matters to make it illegal.

We will always need a police force, and it is the duty of every citizen to help protect the common good by supporting the work of the police. There must be some system of punishment, so that criminals are seen to suffer for their crimes, and so that they can be deterred, forcibly restrained, and encouraged to reform. Nevertheless, systems of policing can sometimes be biased, inefficient or corrupt, and systems of punishment can be vindictive or ineffective. It is also very dangerous for the police to lose the trust of some part of the populace, so great efforts must always be made to ensure co-operation between the police and all parts of society.

The ultimate punishment a society can impose on one of its members is the **death penalty**. The Church, for most of her history, has accepted the right of the state to use this penalty, though she has often pleaded for mercy in individual cases. In recent years, the Church has increasingly opposed the use of the death penalty, and has come to see it *not* as one punishment among others, but as something that may be used *only* when society itself is under threat *and* when society has no other option. The present pope, John Paul II, would reserve capital punishment to 'cases of absolute necessity', which, in a modern penal system, are 'practically non-existent' [*Evangelium vitae* 56]. Thus, if it is possible to keep murderous criminals securely and humanely imprisoned, then it is *never* justifiable to execute them. Every human being is made in the image of God, and society must value the lives even of its criminals, seeing them not simply as destructive or vicious, but also as our brothers and sisters.

THE CRY OF THE POOR

Jesus opened the book and found the place where it was written, 'The Spirit of the Lord is upon me, because he has anointed me to preach good news to the poor. He has sent me to proclaim release to the captives and recovering of sight to the blind, to set at liberty those who are oppressed, to proclaim the acceptable year of the Lord'.
And he began to say to them, 'Today this scripture has been fulfilled in your hearing'.

Luke 4:17–19, 21

God created human beings and gave to them the whole world and all its resources. The primary wealth of the planet – land, water, air, forests and minerals – is intended to benefit *all* human beings. However, so that we may use these resources well and responsibly, it is good for us to be able to claim some things as our own. The Catholic Church holds together these two basic social truths:

- The universal destiny of human goods
- The right to private property

It follows from this that the right to private property cannot be absolute, but has to be limited by other social goods. No one has the unlimited right to abuse or destroy his 'own' property; the community can rightly regulate, tax or redistribute wealth for the benefit of its people, especially the poor; we have no absolute right in justice even to the money we have 'earned for ourselves' – for the creation and sustaining of all wealth depends on co-operation among individuals and on the benefits conferred by the society we live in. Furthermore, there will always be those who cannot find work, or who work as hard as others but have not had the same good fortune or opportunities, and so remain poor. We must grasp the social character of what is called **the common good**.

Social justice involves the fairness of contracts and agreements, the proper distribution according to need of resources such as healthcare, and also the regulation and protection of essentially common goods, such as the environment. Responsibility for justice in society rests not only with the government, but also with all those who make or break contracts, who claim or share resources, or who use common goods.

The particular problems of social justice in the context of modern society have been a concern of the Church since the late nineteenth century. In 1891, in his encyclical letter *Rerum novarum* [literally, 'Of New Matters' – papal documents take their titles from the opening phrase], Pope Leo XIII addressed the subject of workers' rights to form organisations, and to receive a basic wage capable of supporting a family. Since then there have been nine major documents on **Catholic social teaching**. These continue to stress, among other issues, the interests of workers and families, and especially the great evil of mass unemployment.

Governments must respect the principle of **subsidiarity**. Subordinate levels of organisation, such as schools, local councils, workers' associations and family groups, have a right and a duty to take responsibility for their own actions. Decisions should generally be made at the lowest relevant level of government. The central body should limit and regulate the subordinate bodies, to protect the wider common good, but should intervene only occasionally. This is especially true with respect to the fundamental building block of society, the family.

Since the 1960s there has been a growing awareness of injustice in those countries that were once European colonies but are now independent, yet burdened by poverty, debt and political instability. **International justice** must involve the promotion of *peace* and the supporting of *development* in these countries. A new theology has emerged which stresses the need, not simply for development, but also for liberation from injustice. Social injustice is not only due to corrupt individuals; there can be 'structures of sin' that need to be overcome before a just society can be established. At first, Pope John Paul II treated this **liberation theology** with great caution, but later he came to incorporate some of its insights into the Church's social teaching, while rejecting its more extreme tendencies. Another emerging insight is that damage to the **natural environment** is truly a *global* concern, since its causes are often linked to social injustice and its effects often hit the poor first and hardest.

The Church, following the Bible and some ancient philosophers, condemns **usury**, which is the practice of profiting by charging excessive interest on a loan. For a substantial part of the Church's history, the charging of any interest on a loan was forbidden to all Christians; however, since the sixteenth century, some sorts of bank charges – to cover risk, loss, or administration – have been seen as acceptable. The sophistication of the current banking system and money markets has made it enormously difficult to say now what would count as an equitable relationship between lender and borrower; but decisions about investments, loans and repayments *always* remain moral questions and not simply technical questions. The situation of **third world debt**, in which very poor countries are forced to pay off the bad debts of previous governments at high rates of interest, *is* usury, and as such is immoral.

The Catholic Church accepts the right of parents to plan and space the births of their children, and of governments to be concerned about population decline or excessive population growth. However, we must pursue good ends by good means. The Church will not co-operate in encouraging contraception (for the reasons discussed earlier); she strongly opposes programmes of sterilisation and abortion and enforced family size, such as are found in China. She also opposes the bullying of poor nations by rich and powerful ones, or by international bodies. The question of population should not be asked without first addressing the issues of education, peace, political and economic development and environmental awareness.

Catholic social teaching does not provide a complete plan for the perfect society, but it does furnish tools for understanding and implementing justice. In a complex and changing world the Church offers herself as an 'expert in humanity', setting out the goods and values that any system must respect if it is to be called just and civilised.

THE KINGDOM OF GOD

Pray then like this: Our Father who art in heaven, Hallowed be thy name. Thy kingdom come. Thy will be done, on earth as it is in heaven.

Matthew 6:9–10

The aim of the Christian life is to find happiness in friendship with God, by the grace of God. This friendship, which involves faith, hope, and the love of God, also involves a commitment to love our neighbours, and even our enemies, as God loves them. The **kingdom** that we are working for is 'a kingdom of truth and life, a kingdom of holiness and grace, a kingdom of justice, love and peace' [*Roman Missal*]. Therefore we should seek to build a fair and just society, and should care especially for the poor and the socially excluded. Jesus said, 'Whatever you do to one of the least of these, my brothers and sisters, you do to me' [*Matthew* 25:40].

Jesus preached the coming of the kingdom of God, but he also gathered a people together, appointed twelve apostles, and founded the **Church**. Within the Church, we read about the acts and teaching of Jesus in the Gospels, and hear about him in the other parts of the Bible. We also share in the very life of Jesus when we are baptised with water, when we eat and drink his body and blood in the Mass, and when we receive the other sacraments.

The Church is a *visible society* and, in addition to the moral law, she has her own canon law, for the spiritual good of her members. Catholics are bound to fulfil the old Sabbath law by keeping the Lord's day (Sunday), and certain major feasts, as 'holy days' – by going to Mass and abstaining from work that would inhibit rest, celebration or the due worship of God. We are also bound to support the clergy, practise penance at the appropriate times, confess our sins to a priest and receive Holy Communion at least once a year, and marry (if we choose to marry) according to the laws of the Church. Canon law exists to promote our spiritual good, but it cannot of itself bring about unity. It is only the presence of the Holy Spirit that creates the bond of unity and peace.

It is the same Holy Spirit who gives us the hope of really making a difference, and doing something worthwhile with our time on earth. Faced with the immense problems and suffering of the world, and with our own obvious weaknesses, it would be easy to despair, and turn instead to following the crowd, our routine or our immediate impulses. The message of the Gospel is that our hope rests not in ourselves, but in the God who made us and who has already achieved the decisive victory, in the life, death and resurrection of Jesus. Thankfully, it does not rest on our shoulders to save the world, but only to play our part in the great work of God, who is, all the time, healing and redeeming his creation.

The first step for each one of us is to acknowledge the vanity of trying to find happiness on our own, and accept the help that is offered to us. Only by realising the constancy and infinite depth of God's love can we be given the courage to face our failings honestly, confess them explicitly, and, with the help of God, turn from them. Confession and faith in God liberates us to hope, without the dishonesty of pride or self-deception. Then we can ask what plans God has in mind for us, by which we can find happiness through serving others.

Every human being is called to love God and to find salvation, but the particular way of life to which each of us is destined (our calling or **vocation**) is unique. Some are called to great and heroic efforts to preach the faith in the face of danger, or in fighting against injustice for the sake of God's children. No-one is exempt from helping in this struggle; but for many of us the way of life to which we are called will be humble and seemingly ordinary, rather than dramatic. It will be through married life, through teaching music, mending drains, shuffling paperwork, or managing a team of workers, that most of us will find happiness, if it is to be found. What makes each of these works a *vocation* is, above all, the way in which we do it, the love and care with which we live and work with one another, and the honesty of our relationships with God and our neighbours.

We should not think of the moral life as a set of rules that restrict our freedom and stop us from doing what we want to do. We should think of it as the **fullness of life**, the worthwhile life, through which we can find ourselves, and gain a respect for ourselves and for others.

Because of our weakness, this is only possible with God's help, which he gives to us through his Son, Jesus our Saviour, and the Holy Spirit, who is our life and inspiration. Whatever our talents and goals may be, whatever it is that really attracts us (and that we can see to be truly good), we will find fulfilment *only* with God and not apart from him. Rebellion against God is rebellion against reality.

There is a path that God has for us, through which we can find our happiness. What is required of us is to walk this path – not seeing the whole journey, but at every step putting our trust in God. Ultimately all worldly goods will fail, our friends will die, and we too will face death; but if we have trusted in God in life, then we may trust that, even in death, he will bring us to the life of the resurrection, where Jesus awaits us, and where everything we have lost will be restored.

SUGGESTED FURTHER READING

Official Church Teaching

Catechism of the Catholic Church: Part III, Life in Christ; Geoffrey Chapman, Revised edition, 1999

Humanae Vitae, Paul VI (on birth regulation), 1968

Veritatis Splendor, John Paul II (on the fundamentals of morals), 1993

Evangelium Vitae, John Paul II (on the Gospel of Life), 1995

Introductions

Ethica Thomistica, R McInerny (A very nice and readable book); Catholic Univ. of America, 1997

Beyond the New Morality, G Grisez, R Shaw; University of Notre Dame Press, 1988

Life and Death in Healthcare Ethics, Helen Watt; Routledge, 2000

Four Cardinal Virtues, Josef Pieper; University of Notre Dame Press, 1966

Fundamentals of Ethics, John Finnis; Georgetown University Press, 1984

An Introduction to Catholic Social Teaching, Rodger Charles SJ; Family Publications, 1999

Living the Catechism of the Catholic Church – Volume 3: Life in Christ, Christoph Cardinal Schönborn; Ignatius Press, 2001

Useful Reference Works

The Way of the Lord Jesus (three volumes), G Grisez; Franciscan Press (Quincy, IL), 1983, 1993, 1997

The Sources of Christian Ethics, S Pinckaers OP; T&T Clark, 1995

Living the Truth in Love, Benedict M Ashley OP; Alba House, 1996

Healthcare Ethics, Benedict M Ashley OP, K D O'Rourke OP; Georgetown Univ. Pr., 1997

Why Humanae Vitae was Right, Janet Smith; Ignatius Press, 1993

The Abolition of Man, C S Lewis; Harper San Francisco, 2001

Catholic Social Thought: The Documentary Heritage, D J O'Brien & T A Shannon; Orbis (NY), 1992